PRIOR UNITY

First and foremost, people are members of the totality of humankind. Therefore, everyone should actively participate in the global cooperative. That is how it ought to be.

Prior unity is the native state of humankind.

World-Friend Adi Da

We are all part of the one life, the prior unity that expresses itself in myriad ways. This compilation of Adi Da's pointers to the truth speaks to the place in us far beyond the mind. This is a sacred book to be read from the sacred space within us that has never forgotten we have always been one and we can manifest this prior unity on earth straight away.

LISETTE SCHUITEMAKER
Author of *Alight*,
Chair of the Center for Human Emergence (the Netherlands),
Chair of Trustees of the Findhorn Foundation

Prior Unity is a pathbreaking compilation of Adi Da's teachings on planetary non-dualism. Indeed, tribalism, corporatism, and statism are impeding the *external* self-organization of humanity's rules and institutions for meeting the needs of everyone. Yet the *a priori* consciousness of individuality (freedom) and collectivity (equality) already exists as a non-separative unity. Thus, individual and social cooperation can be expressed only through the responsible activism of an embodied, inclusive global community. Let's make it happen!

JAMES B. QUILLIGAN
International economist

Our essential oneness has been emphasized through the centuries by sages. Oneness in *Prior Unity* goes further, elaborating on ego-driven causes of our sense of separateness. This book of readings by Adi Da, compiled by Jonathan Condit, Carolyn Lee, and Leo Burke, highlights the essence for action generating results—knowing we are one, moving from competition to cooperation, being responsible, refusing to play in ego-based, exploitative games. *Prior Unity* inspires us to engage differently in the current context— a profound call to action.

MONICA SHARMA
International expert and practitioner
on leadership development for
sustainable and equitable change

P*rior Unity* provides the wisdom that humanity has longed for to explain the roots of human violence and destructiveness. Every human being who studies this book will re-awaken to the truth, buried in every human heart, that we are not separate individuals, nations, and races, but members of one global family that arises and exists as an egoless prior unity. Read this book, be re-awakened to this truth, and take responsibility, with all seven billion, for the earth and all of humanity as a single system.

—HUGH O'DOHERTY
John F. Kennedy School of Government,
Harvard University

If humankind is going to make it to the other end of this century, it will only be by recourse to great Wisdom-Action. And <u>only</u> together, as Earth-World all together—as one, not two.

Profounder Wisdom is not available anywhere—nor more radical action. Drink from this source—deeply, from its infinite depth.

—ROLF C. CARRIERE
Former UN official,
Senior adviser to Nonviolent Peaceforce

PRIOR UNITY

The Basis For
A New Human Civilization

THE WORLD-FRIEND
Adi Da

Compiled by
Jonathan Condit, Carolyn Lee, and Leo Burke

IS PEACE 723
BETHESDA, MARYLAND

Is Peace 723 is an imprint of the Adi Da Foundation Press
(10319 Westlake Drive, Suite 108, Bethesda, MD 20817 USA)

International Standard Book Number: 978-1-942789-00-0

Library of Congress Control Number: 2015930144

NOTE: Adi Da's communications in this book were adapted by the
compilers following guidelines for such adaptation given by Adi Da
during his lifetime.

CONTENTS

PRIOR UNITY
The Basis For A New Human Civilization

FOREWORD

For over two and a half decades I have taught, coached, and trained people who aspire to be genuine leaders. There are literally tens of thousands of books on leadership, thousands of programs, and hundreds of theories. Many of these tools add value in one way or another. But in all of these years, I have yet to find an approach or method that conveys the full context in which every leader must operate. Amazingly, we have failed to comprehend the ground on which we stand.

In this brief volume, the World-Friend Adi Da masterfully conveys that the world is not only interconnected but, at its root-essence, is a "prior unity", an indivisible whole. He offers this fundamental understanding not merely as a philosophical proposition, but as a direct and straightforward observation, albeit one with profound consequences.

Throughout the ages, mystics and sages have shared the awareness that we are all one. In the twentieth century, physicists discovered that the physical universe is not a solid mass, but an ever-changing, unbroken flow of energy. However, as Adi Da conveys, the force of our outdated assumptions has until now rendered civilization incapable of incorporating these insights into the daily round of human affairs.

We need not go on living in a prison of our own making. People around the world are beginning to step beyond the tired, separative worldview that has generated so much havoc. *Prior Unity: The Basis For A New Human Civilization* offers invaluable wisdom for the transition that is already upon us. It calls for powerful results—all intentionally enacted without any sense of division or opposition. This is not about utopia. It is about the creative, challenging, and long-haul work that requires impactful action, systems shifts, institutional change, and personal transformation.

I am convinced that those who grasp the message of this book—those who really get it—will inevitably be the leaders of the future. This is what the world is calling for. It is now time to get on with it.

—Leo Burke
Director, Global Commons Initiative,
Mendoza College of Business,
University of Notre Dame

INTRODUCTION

The Real Revolution

by Carolyn Lee

A s I write, it is twenty-five years since the fall of the Berlin Wall, on November 9, 1989, the day that thousands of East Berliners poured through the checkpoints for the first time, a human tide that could not be stopped. While reading an article commemorating that event, I came upon a photograph taken at the Berlin Wall the day after it was breached. In the photo, the wall, as yet, is still standing but the people on both sides have climbed up and are reaching over it to shake hands, to embrace each other in celebration.

Photo by Raymond Depardon, courtesy of Magnum Photos

Berlin Wall, November 10, 1989

15

These dazed, excited people have never seen each other before, but there is a recognition happening that is deeper than any outward familiarity. One can feel that, in the joy of the moment, they are no longer East German or West German. They are not even German, first and foremost. With eyes, hands, and hearts caught up in this epiphany of unity and freedom, these men and women have forgotten themselves, and become, simply, human beings—a part of the one body of humanity, recognizing its natural state of relationship and non-separation.

The message of this book, *Prior Unity: The Basis For A New Human Civilization*, needs no better introduction than this iconic photograph. What this book is saying is that the impulse to peaceful, cooperative co-existence is humanity's "true north". This impulse comes from our root-intelligence as one single species, and, at the same time, reflects the inherent unity of all life. We cannot escape the implications. To satisfy what human beings truly want and to ensure a benign future for life on Earth, we have no choice but to transcend what separates us and to build on the deep foundation that we all share, which is our prior, or already-existing, unity.

The World-Friend Adi Da (1939–2008) spoke this message in one way or another throughout his life, seeing and feeling the deteriorating plight of humanity and the Earth. Having lived for many years in Adi Da's Fijian hermitage, I can attest to the fact that he was visibly combined, at profound depth, with the unspeakable sufferings of living beings, while, at the same time, his spiritual state remained utterly untouched by whatever was happening, a perfect demonstration of prior freedom and radiance. This was an overwhelming paradox and a heart-breaking grace to witness.[1]

1. Fuller accounts of the extraordinary nature of Adi Da's spiritual work of "coinciding" with the world can be found in many of his own essays in the final parts of *The Aletheon* (Middletown, CA: The Dawn Horse Press, 2009).

The Meaning of "World-Friend"

The designation "World-Friend" was (to the best of our knowledge) first used by Sri Rang Avadhoot (1898–1968), an Indian spiritual master with whom Adi Da had brief contact while in India in 1968. Adi Da indicated that the reference "World-Friend" became spontaneously true for him in his own case after he received Fijian citizenship in 1993. Formerly an American citizen, he was, at that point, freely established in his hermitage on Naitauba Island, Fiji, having associated, as he put it, "with every dimension of human life—east, west, and indigenous peoples". The title "World-Friend" is indicative of his profound blessing-intention toward the world and all beings, and also suggests his disposition to speak to all in universal "friendship", or as a friend would do, freely and frankly, always founded in deep sympathy and love. ∎

During his lifetime, Adi Da instructed that materials from the archive of his writings and recorded talks (both published and unpublished) should be fashioned into new books on many topics—in addition to the great number of books that he personally created. *Prior Unity* is such a book, compiled after his lifetime but entirely composed of pieces that were written or spoken by him during his lifetime. In considering the contents of this book, I and my colleagues, Jonathan Condit and Leo Burke, explored Adi Da's statements about human culture given over three decades, with the intention of distilling in a small space his compelling argument about what truly human civilization requires. Most of the material comes from his final years, which were marked by an increasing urgency about the state of the world and the necessity for establishing human life on the basis of our inherent, or prior, unity. Virtually every day of 2008 Adi Da offered a torrent of such communication, much of it critical of the human failure to cooperate, but also always full of compassion, inspiration, and, above all, heart-blessing. Even on the last day of his life he gave a discourse calling human beings to rediscover the original human purpose for gathering together in collectives.[2]

Since Adi Da made this observation in 2008, about the then present state of global society, the evidence has become more stark. Vast numbers of people around the world feel that the bottom has fallen out of the social contract that was supposed to provide us with complete security and the opportunity for unlimited participation in our social, cultural, economic, and political life. Instead there is the sense of being indentured to, even threatened by, abstract powers—be they corporations, banks, governments, religious institutions, and so on—which are somehow in control of us and setting the rules with which we are supposed to fall unquestioningly into line. At the same time our deepest security, the planetary environment itself, is being exploited and degraded to an alarming, and unchecked, degree.

How did this happen, and what is the process of rightening? What kind of new, transformed civilization must emerge?

A great conversation, and even fierce debate, about all that is wrong with our society and what must necessarily change is already happening all over the world. Creative ideas and clashes of view are alive in every kind of media and forum, and all over the Internet every day. And so, what is the special contribution of this book?

2. See Adi Da, "Something New Must Emerge", *Not-Two Is Peace*, 3rd ed. (Middletown, CA: Is Peace 723, 2009), 303–8.

To me, the uniqueness of this book lies in the purity and radical nature of Adi Da's message (radical not in the sense of "left-wing", but radical in the sense of "root"). This is not a book about politics as we know it. It is about uncovering the true basis for a new politics, a new social contract that is founded in, and expressive of, how things really are.

The prophetic calling running through the whole book is that if we want to find the real basis for a new human culture we must look beyond the outer world of separate objects, others, and events to the source, the root-condition in which all our experience is actually happening. This is not a religious matter, nor even a spiritual matter in any exclusive sense. It is about the source-reality that has no name, that is not a deity, but which is the being-essence in which we exist, the limitless conscious awareness to which every one of us has access, regardless of our beliefs or philosophy. We do not have to be told, even by scientists, that the quantum level of existence is only light. The human heart intuitively knows this, because it inheres in that light already.

Remarkably, though, this depth of inherent unity is not the place from which we tend to act and live. Something is getting in the way, something so habitual that it has become virtually unconscious. Our awareness of the source-unity of existence is being obstructed by what Adi Da once summarily described as the "myths of ego-culture". Most simply stated, there is only one myth—the presumption of separateness. That myth manifests, firstly, as the presumption that "I" am a separate subjective consciousness, or self, and, secondly, as the presumption that there is a world "out there", which is different from, or other than, the self.[3]

---

3. See Adi Da, "Right Life Transcends The Three Great Myths of Human ego-Culture", *Not-Two Is Peace*, 3rd ed., 203–8. Note that the "third great myth" in the essay is that of separate God, which is not relevant to this discussion.

Of course, this way of perceiving self and world is a natural result of our experience as discrete bodies living in a world of other bodies and things. If we did not perceive the world and others in physically separate terms, we would not be able to operate in space. But the argument on which this book rests is that this perception is fundamentally misleading. At the level of consciousness, it is actually a lie. Consciousness is not divided. Consciousness is the indivisible "stuff" of existence. Consciousness is not separate from anything. The separating is an activity, something we are doing—mentally, emotionally, psychically, and, consequently, in all kinds of concrete physical ways.

This is the activity that Adi Da calls "ego", and it is so deep in our conditioning that we normally never question it. Nevertheless, as he is urgently saying here, the time has come to question it for real.

It is not that waking up to our constant activity of separation will transform us overnight into perfectly enlightened beings. That is not even necessary. The value of such waking up is that we become sensitive to the illusory power of our separate point of view and are no longer bound by that automaticity. A new basis for listening to others and a new platform for action becomes possible—what Adi Da calls the "active disposition", or the "working-presumption", of prior unity.

Are we ready for this? Or does most of humanity have to be developmentally advanced in mental, emotional, psychological, and social terms in order to penetrate, and act beyond, the myth of separateness?

Let us not presume any limitation. There is a mysterious link between the individual and the collective. When a significant experiential change happens in the case of even a few members of a species, then the whole collective of that species may be simultaneously affected. This is the theory of morphic fields, pioneered by the biologist

Rupert Sheldrake.[4] It is a modern scientific indicator of what has been known for thousands of years—that a few can influence the whole (for good or ill), offering further evidence of our intrinsic non-separateness.

Before examining further what the working presumption of prior unity implies, it is worth noting that this presumption is not equivalent to what is generally called "the golden rule", or "do unto others as you would have them do unto you". The golden rule is self-reflexive—it presumes a world of separate others with whom we can cultivate benign co-existence by relating to each and all simply with reference to our own needs and fears. At the global level the golden rule underpins the principle that separate groups, including nation-states, should not act aggressively toward other collectives, because chaos and suffering, to the detriment of everyone, will result.

The evidence of history and the present state of the world give ample proof that the golden rule is not sufficient to maintain peace. It does not get to the perennial root of conflict—the separative reflex. When this reflex takes hold in its collective form, when "I" becomes "we", the deluding, destructive effects of presumed separateness are vastly magnified. Adi Da uses the term "tribalism" to describe this collective ego, or the separative "we". When he refers to "tribalism", he means the psychology of identifying with one's own group first over against all other groups. He is not thereby criticizing the positive bonding between individuals in any human grouping, but pointing to the reflex of separativeness.

How does the working presumption of prior unity become animated in a world where the implacable forces of tribalism appear to rule? Clearly, such a transformation is not going to happen through any mere callings or virtuous admonitions.

4. Sheldrake (1942–) is best known for his 1981 book *A New Science of Life* (reprinted in a new edition in 2009), presenting his theory of "morphic fields", or "morphic resonance".

The force that shapes human consciousness is our lived experience. And so the question arises: What is the context of life that most serves the awareness of our inherent unity? The answer this book proposes is an ancient one—cooperative human-scale community. The felt imperative to create a safe environment that enables people to feel and experience what is greater than mere survival, and to treasure that space in the midst of the fragility of human existence, has always been profound.

However, "community" can mean many different things. What it means in this book is not under-the-same-roof communalism, or anything commonly called "hippie". Adi Da is speaking of the relational handling of fundamental needs by human beings functioning cooperatively in a particular locale. He sees community as the expression of an innate collective intelligence that "pre-solves" the environment in such a way that there is freedom and protection for the unlimited expression of human intimacy and creativity. Rightly established, cooperative community can become the participatory sphere in which unity is self-evident and naturally becomes the law of life, expressed as trust, tolerance, and accountability.

But there is also a built-in danger in the milieu of any community—the danger of tribalism. While a rightly functioning community can provide sanctuary and support for what human beings most deeply want and need, its virtue is betrayed if it becomes a xenophobic refuge against other communities and the wider world.

The challenge posed in this book is to discover how human-scale community can transcend this ancient pitfall and become the template for a global process, whereby the intuitive sense of unity experienced at the intimate scale can become the comprehension of prior unity as a universal truth.

Can we imagine a world whose DNA is the principle of inherent unity and whose cells are inter-connected, fully networked human-scale communities? This vision does not mean one size fits all. Just as the cells of the human body are differentiated according to their position and function, one can envision an integrated human world that would include an infinite variety of cooperative communities, as well as larger groupings of communities, all presuming themselves to be part of a greater regional and global whole.

Can we stand in the place where our primary identity is membership in the community of humanity? Making that real is an immense matter to contemplate. The jump from the local view to the global view seems so great. Our minds move quickly into abstraction when issues no longer touch us directly, but feel far away. Yet, that is exactly where we need to wake up. Feeling that anything not physically immediate to us is far away belongs to our human past, when it was really true. For aeons of time, distance was no small matter, but given modern communications and transport, this is no longer the case. And that is where the argument of this book moves with a relentless logic.

We have no choice now but to take responsibility for the whole planet, and all life within it. This Earth is one ecology existing in one atmosphere, embraced by one indivisible ocean. Every part is a microcosm of the whole and even the Earth itself is barely a speck in the "fractal tree of the universes", as one contemporary physicist put it.[5] Likewise with humanity. We are one species with superficial differences, but fundamentally genetically the same. As homo sapiens, whatever our presumptions of superiority, we are dependent upon the vast inter-connected pattern of life on Earth. This was always true, but now this truth is our only sane and safe basis for global decision-making.

How can such infinite complexity as the whole planet and global human society represent be managed as a totality?

5. Brian Cox, in "Master of Prime-Time Physics" by Tom Lamont, *The Guardian Weekly* 191, no. 21: 32.

In fact, complexity is not the problem, as human beings have demonstrated an astounding capacity for managing complexity when the will is there. The issue, rather, is about coming to a clarity that mandates action.

Global governance based on what works for the totality has never been done, and, in that sense, it represents a revolutionary shift. But that is what this book proposes. In the final essay, "No Enemies", Adi Da introduces his vision of a "Global Cooperative Forum" that would address humanity's common issues on the basis of the well-being of the totality. Based, as it would necessarily be, on the working presumption of prior unity, all the representatives in the Global Cooperative Forum would represent the same thing—humanity and the Earth!

This approach is completely different from that of our current global organizations, such as the United Nations, which start with the presumption of separation, and operate through negotiation between competing interests, hoping to reach agreement—ideally a "win-win" solution to any given problem. But there lies an illusion—the notion that solutions based on trying to reconcile the demands of separate parties can be stable and sustainable. Sooner or later the cracks begin to show, because the well-being of the total picture, which transcends the interests of the bargaining parties, has been ignored. In this paradigm there is no room for the one "win", the win that truly benefits the whole.[6]

The profound reorientation to human issues that Adi Da is advocating depends on us, as humanity, facing the depth of our disillusionment with the old separative paradigm and waking up to a new collective self-awareness. Adi Da coins the term "everybody-all-at-once" to refer to humankind becoming conscious of itself as one species, one family,

6. Adi Da's principal commentary on the Global Cooperative Forum is offered in an earlier book, *Not-Two Is Peace*. As he makes completely clear in *Not-Two Is Peace*, Adi Da is not describing a sudden sweeping away of the prevailing power structures, nor a centralized (and inevitably totalitarian) world-state.

with inherent power to take responsibility for the Earth as a whole. Everybody-all-at-once is suggestive of a unique human coherence, a universal activism that is yet to manifest but is nevertheless already showing signs. As this universal activism gathers momentum, insisting on what humanity as a totality requires, this activism will necessarily manifest an instrument for its purpose—a Global Cooperative Forum. And it may well emerge in a manner that astonishes us with its inevitability, and even suddenness. Like the fall of the Berlin Wall.

The questions implicit in the vision set out in this book are, of course, huge. Identifying and dealing with those questions is the adventure that lies ahead in the real revolution that humanity is crying out for a new human civilization founded not in the destructive politics of exclusion and opposition, but in the peace-enabling power of prior unity. ∎

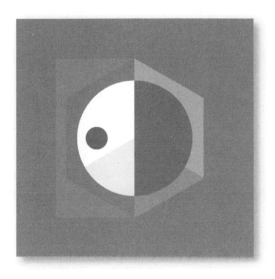

ABOUT THE COVER

Throughout his life, Adi Da worked to develop not only literary but also artistic means of conveying his communication to the world.

The image on the cover of *Prior Unity* was chosen because of its resonance with the theme of the book, and in particular because it suggests the sphere of the planet Earth (the "blue planet") as a prior unity, and the inclusion of the complete rainbow of colors in the image suggests the underlying unity of all apparent differences.

The image is entitled *The Reduction of The Beloved To As Is (The Lover, The Bride, The Wife, The Widow)—Part Four: The Bride / 6*. This image is from the suite *Oculus One: The Reduction of The Beloved*, which Adi Da created in 2006.

Examples of the artwork of Adi Da, together with discussions of his artwork and his own statements about it, may be seen online at:

www.daplastique.com

Something new must emerge.

—Adi Da
November 27, 2008

An Epochal Change Is Required

A global transformation is now required in human culture—after the devastation, or collapse, of ego-civilization in the twentieth century.

Something entirely new is required—something comprehensively right.

My entire life has been spent in working to establish the basis for a "radically" new and "radically" comprehensive culture.

My lifetime of work has always been about the rightening of human existence and the transcending of what is binding human beings and leading them on a destructive course.

What is now required is an epochal change in the history of human endeavor.

A transformation of human understanding and of human processes altogether must occur.

PART ONE

What Must
Be Understood

The world is a prior unity.
It is not that there is a unity yet to be
established, which you must seek for and work on.
Unity is so.

—Adi Da
May 23, 2006

I

The Principle
of Prior Unity

There Is A Universal Conscious Force

There is
   a Universal Conscious Force
That Is
   indivisible,
   egoless,
   acausal,
   and
   absolute.

And everything is arising
   as an apparent modification
   of that.

Reality Itself is
   a prior unity.

Therefore,
   everything that is arising
   is part of
   a prior unity.

It is not just that
   things are connected
   to one another
   in a unified sense.

Everything is arising
   in that which is
   indivisible
   and
   self-evidently Divine.

A Single
Great Principle

Through the entire collective human process
of examining the nature of conditionally manifested
   existence
(including the scientific examination of
   • the development of life-forms on Earth,
   • the origin and evolution of the universe,
      and so on),
a single great principle is made evident:

All manifestation is arising from
a prior and intrinsically indivisible unity.

Everything that appears
is developed from what is already there,
inherently and potentially.

That prior unity
is fundamental to the nature of Reality.

The Presumption
of Prior Unity

The presumption of prior unity—
rather than the conflict between opposing identities—
needs to be the basis for life in human society.

In the larger-picture sense,
life must be lived as that—
instead of the clash of identities,
    or clash of cultures,
    or clash of religions.

The ego-Culture of Separateness
and The egoless Culture of Prior Unity

1.

Humankind is functioning on the principle of ego—or separate identity and separative activity.

Separateness and separativeness—or ego-"I"—is the idea of "difference".

That idea <u>inevitably</u> manifests as the process of "objectification", control, and destruction.

Egos will never unify the world.

Only egolessness (or <u>inherent</u> non-separateness) is the principle of <u>prior unity</u>.

2.

The culture of ego is self-destructive.

A culture of egolessness must emerge. That is a culture of fullness.

The principle of egolessness is the foundation (or root) of the principle of prior unity.

Therefore, the transformation that is necessary is the transformation of human consciousness, individually and collectively, from the principle of ego (or separateness and separativeness) to the principle of egolessness.

The principle of egolessness manifests itself as the <u>active</u> disposition of prior unity.

3.

What is at the end is the same as whatever is at the beginning.

If you begin with separateness, the end is dark.

If you begin with prior unity, all that emerges is light.

Unity Is
A Prior Condition

1.

Prior unity is not about billions of separate egos.

Nor is prior unity about any particular collection of "big" egos.

Prior unity is not about separate bodies of people, each from their own fragment of the world, who come together and are supposed to make a unity out of the persistently presumed dis-unity.

2.

The whole must be (and, inherently, always already is) senior to the parts.

In the current human world, the parts are all self-presumed "absolutes"—each of them (variously) trying either to fulfill itself separately or else to achieve unity with all the "others".

That "paradigm of parts" cannot work.

Only the paradigm of prior unity is right and true—and always fit to work.

When the parts presume themselves to be senior to the whole, the inherent unity of all becomes subordinate to every kind of separate and separative inclination—but when the whole is presumed to be senior to the parts, prior unity becomes the understanding of every one, and all.

3.

Separate-"anythings"-seeking-unity is the principle of falseness.

Separateness cannot achieve unity.

Unity is a prior condition that must enforce itself.

If this is clearly understood, then it will become obvious what must be done, and what must not be done (or allowed to continue), in any particular circumstance.

A New Kind
of Human Consciousness

A new kind of human consciousness
is required—
based on
• the working-presumption
   of prior unity,
and on
• an understanding
   of the indivisibly single world
   in which everyone is living.

This not only involves
the notion that there is such a single world,
but it requires grasping
• the necessity for cooperation,
   and
• the necessity to function
   on the basis of an understanding that
   – the Earth
      is a single system,
      and
   – humankind (likewise)
      is a single whole.

The past pattern of humankind is finished.
The past pattern of humankind must be shed.

—Adi Da
May 31, 2008

11

The History
of Dis-Unity

The Human "Tribes"
Are Face To Face

There are no civilizations any more—in the plural. It is just humankind—in a moment either of terrible potential ending or (otherwise) of the great turnabout that will re-civilize the world on a new basis. What is required is a transformation of humankind-as-a-whole.

Until relatively recently, the human "tribes"[7] were all separate from one another in their geographical zones. Then, over the last two hundred years or so, the "tribes" (more and more) met face to face. Eventually, in the twentieth century, everybody came face to face.

Through the terrible dramas of the twentieth century, all the "tribes" of the world meeting face to face became "tribes" in conflict all over the world, engaging fierce global battles in the mood of separatism and mutual destruction. And, along with that "tribal" conflict, there was the devastation of the Earth-domain. Indeed, the twentieth century brought about the potential of the <u>absolute</u> devastation of both the Earth-domain and the human domain.

Humankind has now reached a turning point. Now a choice must be made to actually stop this devastation. Human beings must stop the "tribally" based war of egos, and enter into the choice of being the total human collective on Earth—with the responsibility to deal collectively and cooperatively with all of the issues that all living beings, in fact, have in common in the Earth-world. Altogether, the entire context of "tribalism" must now be transcended.

What is required is not that the separate "tribes" come out of their separate locations merely in order to engage in

---

7. See the introduction, p. 21, for a description of the meaning Adi Da intends with his use of "tribes".

ecumenical conversation. The "tribes" must realize that, in and of themselves, they are not "absolutes". Each "tribe" represents a tradition that took form in its own time and place, when the "tribes" were geographically separate. Now that they have all come together, looking at one another face to face, every "tribe" is talking as if it is an "absolute", destined to take over the world. How can every one of the "tribes" be an "absolute"?

Humankind, now face to face, must establish a global culture, a global politics, a global society, a global context for humankind—rather than the "tribal" context. The "tribal" context will merely be the basis for struggle and even devastation in the future, because it is controlled by a mind of mythologies rooted in egoity (or the will to separateness). Therefore, the "tribal" context must not be continued. There must be an awakening from it.

Systems of
Identity-and-Difference

The "tribalization" of the human world is based on the ego. Fundamentally, "tribal" structures are systems of identity-and-difference, just as the egoic "self"-image (or ego-"program") is in the case of the individual. Thus, "tribes" (or "tribal" units, or systems of human gathering) are collective systems of identity-and-difference, based (as ego is) on root-separation and root-separativeness.

Being systems of identity-and-difference, "tribal" systems each have their own particular characteristics—including myths (religious myths, historical myths, and so forth), standards of social and ethical (or moral) behavior, expectations relative to behavior (and modes of appearance, and modes of language), and so forth. All of these structures were originally developed in the independent locations of human association. Then they became fixed patterns of identity-and-difference—identity within the "tribe", and difference from those outside the "tribe".

When the world becomes a place of separate "tribes", each associated with its own fixed system of identity-and-difference, then conflict and stress are inevitably produced. The world-situation at the present time is a chaos being created by this confrontation between separate "tribalized" systems, or ego-based systems of identity-and-difference.

However, there is an immediate way to remove the stress from the situation—and that is to have everyone function in a disposition of cooperation and tolerance. Therefore, functioning on the basis of cooperation and tolerance is a fundamental principle that must be established globally—between all individuals, between all nation-states, and between all "tribalized" systems-of-mind of all kinds. That principle must be observed not only within political entities, but within every kind of system of presuming identity-and-difference everywhere.

Out of that obligation to function on the basis of cooperation and tolerance, a new context for human life must emerge. In other words, the old "tribal" systems of identity-and-difference must (at least gradually) be relinquished. And that is a process that is greatly resisted within this "tribalized" world.

People hold on to their "tribal" myths, their "tribal" associations, their "tribal" self-protectiveness, their "tribal" mind, their "tribal" modes of appearance and language, their "tribal" expectations about behavior, and so forth. Human individuals, for the most part, are themselves still embedded in "tribal" mono-cultures—cultures that each have a fixed system of identity-and-difference to which each individual gives allegiance, and with which each individual has (thereby) become identified.

Everybody needs to understand: We do not have to do this any more.

Moral Enlightenment

The awakening from the "tribal" context is what I call "moral enlightenment". The morally enlightened disposition can distinguish between the human accretions of "tribalism" and that which is Real, which transcends temporary human gestures and symbols of the Real (including at the level of politics and ordinary daily-life society).

It is now time for humankind-as-a-whole—everybody-all-at-once—to assume integral responsibility for the human species on Earth. This is really the first time in all of human history that humankind has even been in the position to consider this. Simultaneously, humankind is in the position of having no choice but to deal with it.

The "tribalism" that was carried out of the domains of separate existence must now be thrown into the common fire that everyone tends. Otherwise, the world itself is going to become a conflagration. Therefore, there must be a sacred fire into which everyone throws everything by which human differences might (otherwise) be commanded.

Prior unity is the light of that sacred fire, the guiding source for all rightening in the future. Such rightening is (necessarily) based on humankind existing as a totality—all at once. All forms of "difference" have now effectively been cancelled by the fact that everybody has come into the same room.

Be Part of Humankind First

People must take the position of being part of humankind first. That is the basis for right human discourse, or truly civilized discourse.

That does not mean that you dissociate yourself from your nation, or your birthplace, or your citizenship. Rather, it is about having a disposition that transcends any kind of particularity of orientation—looking at all human problems as part of humankind's collective concern, without any "angle" on anything whatsoever. On that basis, you get down to dealing with the issues in concrete terms, whatever those terms may be relative to any particular issue.

To become part of humankind first is a kind of egolessness. That disposition is not Enlightenment per se, but it is a disposition that transcends the separate and separative "point of view" characteristic of the usual mode of participating in world-business or human happenings.

There are lesser identities that people commonly presume: There is the personal identity—and there is the immediate identity of your associations, your upbringing, your family, your town, your country, your race, your religion, your culture. All of these "point-of-view" images of "self" encumber people's understanding. And these identities are characteristically the first thing that people put out front.

Everyone is play-acting this collection of characteristics of "self"-imagery, this objectified persona that each one tends to identify with. When someone says "I", that persona is who they mean. However, if everyone is part of humankind first, that universal context becomes the basis for examining everything, and it cools all "self"-imagery discourse.

This is how cooperation and tolerance become possible—because people are not wearing their separate identities first. Instead, they are wearing the rather universal identity of being a human being, part of the totality of humankind—participant with all other human beings in simply handling the business that everyone has in common.

Then the handling of business can be focused down to all the particularities, including matters that relate to particular segments of humankind and particular regions of the world. But such (more localized) matters can be addressed in the context of the totality of humankind—rather than in the context of presuming to be a separate and separative identity.

The Old Paradigm
Must Die

People talk about a "new paradigm"—but, all the while, they are actually <u>being</u> the old paradigm.

In that case, any "new paradigm" tends to be just some sort of "costume".

As long as people persist in the old paradigm, they are persisting in "tribalized" ego-culture.

There is no new paradigm until the old paradigm is dead "ground zero".

A whole and new global culture of humankind must be born from this "ground zero".

PART TWO

What Must
Be Done

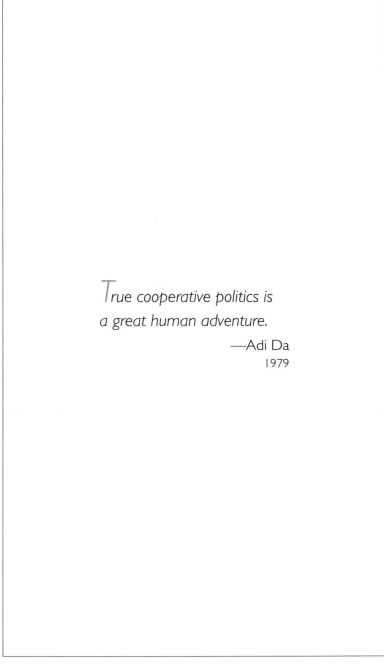

*True cooperative politics is
a great human adventure.*

—Adi Da
1979

III

The Human-Scale Politics
of Cooperative Community

The Retrieval of
Inspired Culture

For the sake of everyone and all, there <u>must</u> now be the retrieval of really and truly inspired culture.

The right and true (and, now and forever hereafter, necessarily <u>global</u>) human culture is, by definition, a universal and positively inspired human domain wherein the possibilities of transcendence and ultimacy are cultivated and developed by <u>all</u>.

The fundamental (and, heretofore, perennial) great disposition that must now be universally retrieved is the disposition to exceed the limitations of mortality, egoity, and gross existence altogether.

That disposition is the right and true and necessary domain of right and true culture.

The world culture of humankind as a whole needs to become re-oriented now—away from its "meditation" on the downward spiral into darkness and the myths of "end-time", and profoundly toward the disposition that would transcend <u>all</u> limitations.

Vibratory Participation

There is a human necessity
for a kind of resonation
of vibratory participation
    in Reality
        (Itself, and altogether),
    and Truth
        (Itself, and altogether),
    and Beauty
        (or the Beautiful,
        Itself, and altogether)—

    beyond conventional "yes" and "no",
    beyond conventional "beauty"
        and conventional "ugliness",
    beyond conventional "realism",
    and
    beyond egoity altogether.

Such human profundity
is a great and necessary purpose,
which true culture and right civilization
should and must serve.

The Urge To Participate

The fundamental urge of humankind-as-a-whole is to participate—not to be shut down, not to be thrown back on themselves, not to be treated merely as consumers who want this, that, and the other thing.

People want the opportunity of participation.

All over the world, the energy of participation is what should be tapped.

Instead of addressing everybody in terms of their problems, their "self"-interest, their consumer mentality, their egoity, address them as people who are patterns of energy wanting to participate.

The human world is an energy of participation.

Therefore, it needs a pattern by which people can participate.

The pattern must be provided.

The Impulse of
Cooperative Union

C ommunity, or cooperative acculturation, is the self-fulfilling urge of humankind.

It is the duty and natural, spontaneous impulse of already free men and women to create a cooperative union with other human beings. Community, in this sense, is the only human politics. In all other politics, something other than humankind is made the principle.

In traditional and past times, community was a principal invention of humankind. People knew that they could not survive as a mass of isolated individuals, but only in communities, or forms of cooperative order that were always growing toward a more and more stable and local "pre-solution" of fundamental and common problems or needs.

In time, forms of group-consciousness were magnified, so that great abstracted polities began to replace the local and human associations.

However, the process of community cannot take place in great abstract, parent-like institutions. Such institutions can at best reflect that process. Rather, the process of community must take place at the intimate level of ordinary human life.

Nevertheless, in the present era of urbanization, human beings have tended to imagine that community is no longer necessary. Therefore, they live in isolation, appealing to the "parent" nation-state for the benefits of survival.

This illusory order is beginning to strain and disintegrate—it is becoming clear again that the people must take responsibility for their own common life.

Cooperative, Human-Scale Community

Civilization always originates as an expression of the ideals of cooperative, human-scale community.

Therefore, whatever the present-time particular, distinguishing characteristics of any civilization may be, the principal characteristics that stand at the root of any civilization (and, therefore, of the present civilization) are those of cooperative, human-scale community itself.

And those characteristics are, basically, the political, social, and cultural motives and practices of cooperation, interrelatedness, interdependence, non-competitiveness, true (or positive, rather than merely insipid) harmlessness, and positive (or ego-transcending, and other-serving, rather than merely "self"-negating) "self"-sacrifice.

The key to this is love.

Love is ego-surrendering, ego-forgetting, and ego-transcending participation in the indivisible oneness and wholeness and singleness that is Reality Itself.

Therefore, love is also right living.

And that love which is right living is not ego-based, independent, separative, competitive, and non-cooperative.

Therefore, that love which is right living is the active (and co-operative) aspiration toward egoless (or non-separative) participation in Reality Itself, and in relational humanity, and in even all the all there is.

The "Food" of Life

I n a rightly functioning community, people share life itself
in the form of principal "food":
- intensity,
- energy,
- love,
- light,
  and
- Consciousness,
all in the form of
- "self"-sacrifice,
  or
- mutuality.

No Longer Exploitable

In a true cooperative human community, every one knows what every one else has the <u>tendency</u> to become (when irresponsible) and the <u>possibility</u> to become (when responsible).

And all serve one another at the level of <u>that</u> understanding.

They all also know the functional character and capability of each one among them, and they amuse and enjoy and serve and employ one another at every appropriate level.

Right <u>responsibility</u> for functional life (and, thus, for the positive unifying of the structures of the human individual, and of all the members of the human collective itself) must always be assumed and demanded in a truly human (or truly ego-transcending, and cooperative, and mutually tolerant) community.

When it is not, that failure of responsibility (and, thus, of individual well-being and of collective unity) will, inevitably, weaken the community—and, thus, enable (or even oblige) shrewder men and women to exploit and oppress the members of the community, and make them slaves to their own egoity again.

If men and women will enter into <u>true</u> cooperative human community—and, therefore, into intimate cooperative and higher cultural relationship with one another—they will no longer be exploitable by any life-negating (or disheartening and freedom-negating) influences from the abstract social and political realm of the worldly "news".

The negatively dominant bureaucracy of the world of egos becomes obsolete only through non-use.

And, once its negative and parent-like powers become obsolete through non-use, even the State will be obliged to become the simple instrument of the responsible agreements of the people.

If the people become truly intelligent and freely cooperative, then the State will, inevitably, do (or become) likewise.

And if the people truly become collectively intelligent and responsible, then individual freedom can never really be eliminated by the state of the "news".

The Fundamental Domain
At The Center of Life

1.

Human beings are not alive on Earth merely to be cogs in the machine of hoped-for progress toward utopia—merely to sing their "cricket song",[8] make a baby or two, and then drop dead. No. There is also the impulse based on the knowledge that this human birth is a mortal condition. It is the urge to find what is greater, and to be included in that.

Every living being has the instinct of Infinite Life. That instinct, that urge, must be allowed, cultivated, even educated.

2.

It is not enough merely to get up every morning and go to bed every night, devoting the hours between waking and sleeping to nothing but functioning. Such practical functioning has no ultimacy to it. It is similar to a computer language— it is simply a program designed for certain limited purposes.

If human culture becomes such that it renders human existence entirely profane, or secular—not even allowing or suggesting that people "reach beyond"—that is a terrible situation. But that situation is not uncommon for human beings, and it is not unique to this "late-time" (or "dark" epoch). Generally speaking, people seem to be fixedly focused on gross matters and possibilities—everything associated with gross human life. And, generally speaking, human intelligence is brought to bear primarily on gross matters, gross problems. In this "late-time" (or "dark" epoch), all else has been defamed or misrepresented—to

---

8. Adi Da uses the phrase "cricket song" as a metaphor for being content to live life in an "automatic" manner, simply living out the patterns of an ordinary life, without doing anything more profound.

such an extent that it has become the common set of mind either to ignore the domain of the sacred (and the Ultimate, or the Divine) or to presume that it is nonsense.

Even when scientists (who are, generally speaking, part of the secular culture of the gross-physical orientation) speak in paradoxical (and potentially sacred) language about the nature of reality as it is being presumed from a scientific and mathematical "point of view", there is no corresponding sacred culture called for or suggested. If reality is the non-dual paradox suggested even by twentieth-century physics, then where is the sacred human culture of truly participatory existence that corresponds to such a universe? No such culture is—in general—being proposed or created. Rather, the general presumption seems to be that everyone is supposed to be a mere worker of some kind, devoted to progress toward some imagined social utopia, some political design to be achieved in the future (for whomever, whenever), and ignore profound matters—ignore not only profound <u>questions</u>, but profound <u>doings</u>. Such doings are the right occupations of human beings—doings that take seriously the culture of "reaching beyond", together with the right handling of gross life.

Everything in the sacred domain is about ecstasy. Everything in the social (or secular) domain is about control of ecstasy and using the principal human faculties (of body, emotion, mind, and breath) for other (generally, non-ecstatic—or ego-based) business in the moment. The basic taboos of the secular social domain are against sex (or bodily pleasure altogether), laughter (or genuine humor, and mental freedom), and Real-God-Realization (or Ecstatic Identification with the Divine Reality). From the "point of view" of the secular social domain, sex, laughter, and Real-God-Realization must be controlled, because they are forms of ecstasy—and because the social-personality world feels threatened by the lack of social "self"-control implicit in ecstasy. Within the context of the secular social domain, such "self"-control is appropriate, and even necessary, for the purposes of conducting ordinary human business. There should be certain forms of "self"-control (or social "self"-discipline) in that domain of practical interaction between people. It is just that the world of human activity and experience must not be reduced to being only that practical (or secular) domain.

The sacred domain must be the core of life, and all kinds of activities and experiences belong there that do not belong in the secular social domain—but you must be able to enter into the sacred domain, readily, and be there when you get up in the morning, and freely enact there all the forms of ecstasy that you do not enact in the common (or secular) daily domain. The sacred culture determines how the forms of ecstasy are accommodated in human life, whereas the secular social world always wants to exclude them. If you have nothing but the secular social world, then ecstasy in all its forms—even sexual—becomes suppressed, its integrity destroyed. Then life becomes nothing but a "self"-conscious exercise in which you merely preserve social rules, extending them even into the bedroom and the prayer room—such that you never turn ecstatic, you never "go native", when you are outside the common social (or secular) sphere.

Sex, laughter, and Real-God-Realization have their place in the sacred domain, at the center of life. The secular (or public) dimension of human existence should be economized, kept in its proper place, not allowed to take over the entirety of your life. There must be a sacred core of life, a culture at that core. And everything that has to do with ecstasy should be in that sphere, not in the secular (or public) sphere.

The sacred domain is about the expression of ecstasy—in all its forms. Therefore, all the arts—and, indeed, all forms of creativity—are, basically, about the sacred domain.

Everything about right religious and Spiritual life (including meditation, worship, prayer, and so on) is in the sacred domain. The sacred domain is even the primary place of food-taking. The sacred domain is the place of emotional-sexual intimacy, the place of friendship and human intimacy altogether. The sacred domain is the place where the truly human (and humanizing) culture of ecstasy is truly practiced, in the truest sense, assisted by cooperative association between people.

3.

The sacred should be the fundamental domain of everyone's life. It is in everyone's interest to protect the sacred domain and see that it flourishes in all its forms—for everyone, all over the world. Everyone should have access to the sacred domain—otherwise, a collective insanity, or lack of sanity, develops. That lack of sanity comes from having lost touch with what is beyond oneself—or the Sea of Divine Existence, altogether.

4.

Giving people the means and the opportunity to be focused in the sacred domain is very basic to the creation of truly cooperative human community.

The reason so much of human existence is out of control in this "late-time" (or "dark" epoch) is that the sacred (and, therefore, truly cooperative) forms of life have been almost destroyed. The dimensions of human existence that rightly belong in the sacred domain have been forced into the secular (or public) domain, where they cannot rightly flourish. When people no longer have a true anchor in the free, sacred domain, then they become aberrated in the common sphere of secular restraints. The prevailing trend, in this "late-time" (or "dark" epoch), is to secularize everything in the human sphere, and to reduce everything to the "point of view" of "matter-only". This is a false and terribly destructive "point of view".

The restoration of the sacred domain is the means for creating human balance in the world again. Only sacred culture gives people the means to live a truly sane existence. Ecstasy is a human necessity. This must be accepted and agreed by all. Thus, the creation of truly cooperative human community is not merely desirable for the sake of ordinary social human functioning, but the creation of truly cooperative human community is, itself, a profound <u>necessity</u>—because it is the means for establishing the sacred domain (and the ecstatic disposition) at the center of the life of <u>every</u> human being

The Fundamental
Human Urge and Need

The fundamental human urge and need
is not food, sex, power, "things",
or even physical survival.

The fundamental human urge and need
is happiness—
but not in the mere "satisfaction-of-self" sense.

The fundamental human urge and need
is <u>ecstasy</u>.

Humankind-as-a-whole must establish the principle of prior unity on a global scale.

—Adi Da
April 30, 2008

I V

Responsibility
For The Global Totality

The Whole
Must Manage Itself

The general situation of humankind-as-a-totality is treated as a remarkable exception, when compared to all the other things that human beings do. Virtually every kind of association between people comes to be organized, or put into some kind of workable order. Even the bodily human individual does certain things, sets certain limits, has a certain understanding of how to function—just in order to survive. Thus, every kind of association between people—a household, a family, a village, a county—has its laws. And any larger form of human association has its mayors, its councils, its boards, even its modes of law enforcement and court systems, and on and on.

Every kind of human collective is made subject to agreements, limits, laws, rules, and means of keeping it straight, productive, and positive—except for the totality of the human world.[9] The totality is made an exception in this regard.

Humankind-as-a-whole is not managing itself. Instead, humankind-as-a-whole is managing all of its separate, rather "tribalized" elements—and it puts together various coalitions among those elements, over against other coalitions. Humankind-as-a-whole enacts that sort of self-organization of its separate elements—but the world-as-a-totality is organized (or not organized) on the basis of competition, on the basis of presumed "difference".

The global totality is allowed to be a place of mere competition—without an instrument of order applied to the whole. Thus, the global totality is the only domain of human collective existence that is made an exception to what is

9. See "The Global Cooperative Forum" (pp. 99–100) for an explanation of why Adi Da did not regard such bodies as the United Nations as truly performing the function of managing the whole.

otherwise the rule of how people function. This is so because another principle has been traditionally presumed about how the human totality is supposed to work. The totality is supposed to be based on warfare, competition, mutual struggle, dominance of one over another. It is a kind of "wilderness" idea.

Just a few centuries ago, people thought that if you went outside of your domain, you first of all entered into a wilderness of beasts and devils, and then you fell off the edge. The presumption that the whole is a wilderness—and, therefore, a place where you cannot or should not go—is actually the mythology that is being applied by human beings globally relative to the totality of Earth and the totality of human existence. It is presumed that, because the totality is a wilderness, human beings do not have to be responsible for it—they just need to avoid it.

It is presumed that the wilderness is intrinsically about chaos—whereas every other human domain is presumed to be necessarily subject to being put in order, with necessary responsibilities to be maintained by human collectives. Every domain of human existence is subject to the rule of order—except for the whole.

It is the same now relative to the mythology of outer space. Human beings have not gone out into space enough to presume that they are responsible for the order of the galaxies. Maybe that will change at some point. But, for now, outer space is presumed to be a kind of wilderness outside the sphere of human control and responsibility.

However, the Earth-world is no longer a wilderness. Especially since the nineteenth century—and even before that, when European explorers first went around the world and mapped it, and then, more and more, with the advent of industrialization and advanced modes of communication and travel—the world cannot properly be thought of as a wilderness. Instead, it is now self-evident that the world is like your local village or town or county or state or nation. It is a place that must be put in order.

For the world-as-a-totality to be put in order, a new kind of human institution must be in place. To create such an institution eliminates the mythology of the totality being a wilderness, and (instead) makes the totality into a domain of human responsibility. This shift is absolutely essential.

"Tribalism" must be replaced by the presumption of prior unity. Gross competition must be replaced by the presumption of prior unity. War is simply the grossest form of competition. Indeed, the daily life of human beings, managed in what is essentially a global warrior-culture, is basically about competition. The world must no longer be treated as a wilderness, in which competition is enacted through war and competition for resources. Instead, there must be a global cooperative that brings fundamental order to human life on Earth.

All of the terrible happenings in the world are due to the failure to understand that the world-as-a-whole is now like your local village. Cooperative responsibility has become an absolute necessity.

The world is not a place for vast competitions between huge nation-states and coalitions of nation-states. That is the "tribal" view of the world—the view that, if you walked a little too far outside your village, you fell off the edge of the Earth, or the view that what is "out there" is simply monsters. All of that is part of the political mythology of day-to-day life. The monsters are always the other nation-states, the ones that are not in your coalition.

In reality, there are only human beings everywhere—and it is human beings that must be collectively responsible for the global situation of humankind. That responsibility covers all matters at the physical level of human life.

Humankind must accept the responsibility for its self-management at the level of totality. It is simply a change in consciousness that is required—a change that should be rather automatic, if people would just wake up and look at what is happening in the world.

Humankind-as-a-whole will not accept responsibility for the world-totality until it wakes up to the fact that the totality is, indeed, an area of necessary human responsibility, rather than a wilderness of necessary human conflict. Thus, the idea of prior unity is not really an <u>idea</u>, but is (rather) an <u>observation</u>. Prior unity is simply the nature of Reality Itself, demonstrated as the totality of humankind. That totality is intrinsically a unity. And that unity must be institutionalized as a cooperative of self-managing human responsibility, like any other area of human concern or enterprise.

The Big Picture
and The Small Picture

1.

The same issues pertain at the individual level that pertain at the global level. They are about the same pattern. Self-management must be established at the individual scale, just as it must be established at the collective and global scale. Thus, the big picture and the small picture are one picture. They are hand-in-glove with one another, and must be understood as such.

Global imbalances are a reflection of individuals. At the global scale, everyone is aware of pollution and climate change and extreme weather patterns, and so forth. However, people are less aware of how such global issues are a reflection of what human beings are doing individually and how the system is controlling people negatively. The same system is producing both pollution of the Earth-world and pollution of the individual body. It is all one pattern. The structure of "tribalized" nation states, corporate power, and big financial interests is the mechanism whereby the Earth is being polluted. It is also the mechanism whereby individual bodies are being polluted.

2.

There are two forms of dependency that have been globalized, and which must be gone beyond—two that are of fundamental global importance. One is dependency on fossil fuels, and the other is dependency on animal protein. Both of these have broad political, social, and economic implications associated with the large conglomerates of corporate power—in association with governments, lobbying of governments, and so on.

Dependency on fossil fuels is having a global effect relative to climate change and extreme weather, plus various other economic matters and problems in international relations. Similarly, the dependency on and exploitation of animal protein is also having a significant effect on climate change—both from the transmission of methane into the atmosphere (a natural byproduct of the animals themselves) and from the use of fossil fuels in the animal-protein industry. The huge consumption of water by the animal-protein industry is also an issue.

Dependency on animal protein is having an effect on individuals—and, in fact, on mass populations—relative to toxic living in general. The implications of the animal protein issue are global, not just personal. Generally speaking, people tend to see fossil-fuel dependency as a larger global issue, but they tend to think of animal-protein dependency largely as a personal issue. In fact, both forms of dependency have everything to do with the entire range of issues from global to personal.

In addition, meat production is an industry that has created immense suffering on Earth. There are billions upon billions of animals not only slaughtered but gravely mistreated by animal industries all over the world every year.

3.

Fossil fuels and animal protein are two key modes of material exploitation of the Earth-world and of humankind. They are of equal significance, and they are inextricably related to an entire range of other problems. Both of these forms of dependency are held in place by governments and massive corporations—and, in relation to fossil fuels in particular, there are people who will argue that even global economic stability depends on this form of dependency being maintained.

In the domain of government currently, there is some sense that fossil fuels must be replaced by alternative forms

Conscious Light Is The Reality For All

As a human being, recognizing the prior unity of the world, you must have concern for Earth itself, and all the species within it, all life within it, all structures and forms and processes that are part of the world, including all the non-humans.

This does not mean one should view non-humans as if they were humans. Rather, this means one should view humans as part of a larger whole. The same Conscious Light is the Reality for all and the State of all. That is the basis for considering issues that have to do with non-humans as well as humans.

Human beings have the ability to conceive and voice issues that relate to the Earth and to the non-human species. On that basis, human beings must address issues that relate to the Earth and non-human species, and human beings must do so rationally and compassionately. ∎

of energy. Thus, there is some movement in that direction, although it is nowhere near the speed it needs to be in order to handle the effects of the continued use of fossil fuels at every level of the Earth-domain—not just climate change, but an entire spectrum of other effects, economic and political. But there is virtually no general consciousness at the level of governments—or even at the level of public knowledge—of the devastating effect that the consumption of animal protein (and the industrialization of meat production) has on human health. People should have access to pleasurable ways of maintaining life through an optimum diet. For the well-being of the planet and for optimum human health, it would be good if everyone adopted a diet rich in green foods.[10] While this is not going to happen overnight, this shift can certainly be served through availability of healthy foods (including support for the growing of such foods) and through education about diet and natural health practices.

4.

I am not trying to replace the current world-situation with a utopia. Utopia is not what this world is about.

Nevertheless, there can be right life and self-managed responsibility, individually and collectively in cooperation— all the things that make a life into a positive endeavor, in the midst of inevitable suffering and limitations.

For that to be the case at the level of humankind-as-a-whole, there must be change at the level of government (or politics) and at the level of corporate behavior and at the level of collective behavior of all kinds.

5.

It is essential that humankind-as-a-whole get off now-obsolete forms of fuel. The world is being overwhelmed with its own waste and the toxicity of what it is ingesting at every level, from industrial to personal. And that is essentially the root of the current world-situation—dependency on bad energy-sources.

There must be a greening of the body, as well as the greening of the planet. There must be a different kind of ecology of human existence—not just in the environment, but in the body of each individual. In this process, everyone would participate in cooperative structures that enable them, through their own action, to generate survivability and well-being for everybody—from the local domain to the global totality, and from the totality to the local.

10. See Adi Da, *Green Gorilla* (Middletown, CA: The Dawn Horse Press, 2008), 63–73.

"Zero-tox", or "No-tox", is what it is about—getting off toxicity dependency, both at the level of the individual body and at the level of the global environment. To bring this about, there needs to be a transition to new life-giving technologies—going beyond the past and making use of what is now possible. This includes new forms of fuel at every level, from personal to collective to Earth-world-as-a-whole. That is the essential issue in broad terms. What is required is a combination of new government and corporate policy plus individual activism based on knowledge of the facts.

The "Everybody Force"

1.

For fundamental positive change to happen in the world, the world of everybody (all-at-once) must represent itself (all-at-once).

The world of everybody (all-at-once) must get out of the position of passively accepting guidance and receiving calls to virtue. The world of everybody (all-at-once) must accept the necessary position of taking control of the world-situation. That is what must happen—or else there can no longer be any hope of a cooperative world at peace.

2.

Political and cultural leaders are not, themselves, going to be able to make this change occur. Such a profound degree of change cannot be brought about by the virtuous voice alone. Rather, such a profound degree of change can only be brought about by the force of humankind as a collective whole, or the "everybody force". The inherent collective of everybody-all-at-once actually is (always) the only true power—but that collective is not currently exercising that power, because that collective is dis-united and in chaos.

3.

In the present-day, the culture and politics of illusion controls the world. The underlying idea that personal and collective egoic "self"-fulfillment is what life is supposed to be about is the root-source of the current global chaos. As a result, there are billions of human individuals (and, otherwise, large numbers of competitive and mutually dissociative groups, cultures, traditions, races, religions, corporations, and nation-states) that are, characteristically (and even strategically), out of touch with each other—like dust, and bombs, and petty traffic, all blowing in the wind. That wind steadily blows all prior unity into the bits and particles of human chaos.

4.

Merely calling on everybody to establish peace and rightness does not create the desired result. To call the chaotic world of egoic human individuals to establish peace and rightness is like trying to give verbal instruction to a cat. Generally speaking, cats do not take verbal instruction—nor do cats respond to advice, or callings, or guidance, or being told what to do at all. They simply do not <u>do</u> that.

That is also how it is with the world of humankind. The world of fragmented individuals and impenetrable collectives is neither available nor amenable to be advised, or called upon, or instructed. However, the world as everybody-all-at-once <u>is</u> (inherently) in a position to collectively decide that things are going to be rightened. The condition of the demand for rightness must be established as reality by the collective of everybody-all-at-once.

5.

If human beings collectively (as everybody-all-at-once) realize that they are (always already) in a condition of <u>prior</u> <u>unity</u>—and, therefore, of <u>necessary</u> co-existence and mutuality—with one another, and if, on <u>that</u> basis, they stand firm together, then they will be in a position to <u>directly</u> righten the world-situation. The collective of all the billions of people <u>can</u>—and, indeed, <u>must</u>—refuse to go on with the current chaos.

However, this profound shift will not occur simply because the billions of humankind are advised, or called upon, to do so. The billions of individuals—as billions of egos—are not going to respond to any such advice or calling, because they are too busy indulging themselves in the marketplace of personal, social, religious, scientific, and political illusions. Therefore, the egoless everybody-all-at-once must open their eyes, see for real, relinquish their helplessness, and take direct responsibility for the human world-event. The egoless everybody-all-at-once must renounce its illusions and "come out of the closet" as the only "we" of planet Earth.

6.

Fundamental (or all-rightening) change cannot be caused. However, fundamental change can <u>happen</u>—as a spontaneous (and all-transforming, or all-reforming) self-conversion. Also, the necessary self-conversion that is required for fundamental change to occur can, itself, be <u>enabled</u> to happen—not by causing it as effect (as if it were already not-existing, and, therefore, needs to be "created out of nothing"), but, most simply and directly, by re-empowering the self-organizing integrity and prior unity of the inherently egoless everybody-all-at-once that <u>already</u> <u>exists</u>.

It will not be the role-playing of "virtuous speaking" that brings about the necessary fundamental change. Calling everybody to change does not cause them to change. Those who are already moved to do right do not need to be told to do so—and, no matter how much advice and admonition they are given, those who are not inclined to do right are not going to "change their act".

If there is going to be fundamental all-rightening change, something has to <u>require</u> change. Therefore, the world as a whole must be enabled to require change. It is an acausal matter—not a causal matter.

7.

The really-existing inherent collective of humankind has inherent power. The "everybody-all-at-once" has the inherent characteristic (and integrity) of <u>prior</u> <u>unity</u> <u>and</u> the inherent capability (and integrity) of a self-organizing principle. Power in the hands of a few cannot manipulate the total collective, if the total collective exercises its inherent power of prior unity and self-organizing energy.

It is not that "the people" (as some kind of immense natural ego) is morally virtuous, and should, therefore, "take over the world" through some kind of "mob rule". Only more chaos can come from more ego-power. Therefore, it must be asked, where is true moral virtue? True moral virtue is only at the inherently egoless root-context of existence.

8.

Whenever human awareness is subordinated to the inherently egoless (and, thus, non-separate and non-separative) root-context of existence, human life becomes morally enlightened (in both voice and action) by the radiant virtue of selflessness. Therefore, if everybody-all-at-once is represented and mobilized by morally-enlightened principles and persons, Reality Itself has re-acquired the voice and ability to make right changes.

9.

It is only the presumption of egoity (or the illusion of inherent separateness) that makes the billions of humankind enact separation from one another—and, thus and thereby, they refuse to enact mutual tolerance, peaceful coexistence, and universal cooperation with one another. In Reality, the billions of humankind are not separate from one another— and should not act to achieve, affirm, or, in any manner, presume separation from one another. In Reality, the billions of humankind exist in the root-context of egoless prior unity. If the inherent energy of that egoless prior unity were brought to the fore, it would spontaneously take responsibility for self-rightening the world.

10.

What is (inherently) egoless must re-assert its inherent power in the world. The Reality-power of everybody-all-at-once existing in the condition of prior unity is what must re-assert itself. When humankind as a whole functions in the disposition of prior unity, a positive order is initiated and (inevitably) self-organized. That can (and must) be done.

Chaos has come about because everything became individuated—every "thing" and every "one". When everybody is fragmented into separate units, there is inevitable chaos. However, when everybody starts to function on the working-presumption of egoless prior unity, then there is the means to bring order into the world of human experience. It is an egoless matter. And, therefore, it is not a religious matter (in the sense of being determined by the dogmas of a particular religious tradition)—but it is a perfectly serious matter (in the sense of being an articulation of inherently egoless, indivisible, absolute, and infinite Reality Itself).

11.

As egos, the billions of humankind are simply a mob of individuals—and that is chaos. However, the billions as an egoless (or indivisible and cooperative) presence is something entirely different. The inherently egoless presence of everybody-all-at-once does not (in order to be re-asserted) require that it, first, be caused—or become the "idealistic" result of some kind of process whereby each individual must first, and one by one, become an egoless perfectly Enlightened being. No—the inherently egoless presence of everybody-all-at-once already (or priorly) exists—and, therefore, it need only be "realistically" self-asserted.

12.

Everybody-all-at-once must become dis-illusioned with the ego-made chaos of the present-time world-situation.

That dis-illusionment can make everybody-all-at-once effective in the true Reality-situation of life.

That dis-illusionment can set the energy of everybody-all-at-once in motion, free of the structures and purposes of ego-bondage.

That dis-illusionment is the root and necessary basis for the awakening of everybody-all-at-once to the inherently global responsibility of humankind.

The People and The Corporations Must Re-Civilize The World

Corporations and businesspeople around the world are, in actuality, more powerful than governments. Corporations can effect the necessary changes in the world. They can do it—instead of creating the situation as it now is.

If such people would enter into an alliance with one another, they could transform politics—virtually overnight, immediately. But they must get together, and they must get collectively behind some ideas that are clarifying (such as the communications I am making), and do it—not just buzz together, and basically try to protect their own status and wealth.

The point is not for them to destroy their own wealth. I am not suggesting that. But they must discover a new model for how to make use of wealth and the power associated with wealth.

All the corporate power that exists around the world can be made cooperative, linked together. It crosses national boundaries, idealisms, and all the rest of it. The collective power of all the corporations (the dominant financial forces and economic forces, and the institutions associated with those forces) and the collective power of all the people in the world, all of humankind altogether—these are the great strengths that can (and must) be used. These are the means that can righten the current trend toward the otherwise inevitable death and destruction of civilization, and of humankind altogether, and of the entire Earth-world.

The corporations and the people are what should be appealed to—not nation-states, and not traditional institutions of religion. This is where the power is. The power is in the people-as-a-totality, and in corporate-wealth-and-power-as-a-totality. That is where the real power is.

That is what can make the change. Therefore, that is what must be mobilized to re-orient nation-states (and the people within them) to rightness—to re-civilize the world, not to degrade the world further.

Corporations as they are now functioning are degrading the world altogether, and they are the reason why nation-states have taken on the anti-civilization form they have. Therefore, corporations must correct themselves and be accountable to greater principles.

The power is in the totality of the people and in money. Through the right action of those who have money—along with the totality of the people speaking plainly and making righteous demands—everything can be turned around, and all problems can be addressed in a rational and civilized manner. Lay it all out on the table, and see what is already right and what needs to be the subject of making agreements. That is what should be done—and always free of any form of threatening the people.

The Only Potential Civilization
That Can Survive

People from all directions, with all of their capabilities and expertise—including people who have political or organizational capabilities—all have their part to play in taking responsibility for the global totality, but the intended focus of any gathering for that purpose must be cooperation and dealing with the business of humankind.

In any such gathering, those participating must actually be there on the basis of presuming prior unity, representing the purposes of humankind-as-a-whole, not particular nation-states and traditions.

Nation-states and traditions do not have to be destroyed, in terms of cultural identities.

They do not have to disappear—although, in fundamental terms, they have already largely disappeared.

But nation-states and traditions are not the point.

They must no longer function as the basis for separation and non-cooperation.

There are universal principles that now apply—principles of cooperation and tolerance, rooted in the working-presumption of prior unity—and those principles apply to all.

A civilization based on those principles is the only potential civilization that can survive.

There is just one world here, one Earth,
one mass of humanity.
All the divisions and conflicts between
the separate "somethings" no longer apply.

—Adi Da
June 1, 2006

V

The Politics
of Prior Unity

The Global Cooperative Forum

A Prefatory Note
to Adi Da's Essay "No Enemies"

*I*n the following essay, the World-Friend Adi Da calls
for a new global process, which would, in his words, give
*"governing force" to the principle of prior unity. How is this
to come about? It requires, as he says, "an instrument" that
would enable global humanity to become self-organized and
self-managed. He names this yet-to-be-realized instrument
the "Global Cooperative Forum".*

*The necessity for such a Global Cooperative Forum rests
on the fact that no presently-existing global organization is
equipped to truly deal with the complexity of the world situation. While global organizations, such as the United Nations,
were established after the Second World War, they have been
unable to function effectively for the well-being of the whole
because of the prevailing paradigm—which is that of separate parties negotiating settlements that maximize their own
self-interests. The global good (both human and non-human)
is thereby subordinated to the aims of the separate parts.*

*In the current world, human beings are simply suffering
this situation, or exploiting it, or both. Therefore, a shift of
consciousness is essential, from the mind of separateness and
competition to taking responsibility for the whole.*

In this essay, and (in more detail) in his book Not-Two
Is Peace, *Adi Da describes how the Global Cooperative Forum
would be the expression of "everybody-all-at-once"—meaning
the unique force and potential in humankind when it wakes
up and becomes aware of itself as one family, even one
"system", existing in unity with (and responsible for) the entire
Earth-system.*

Such a Global Cooperative Forum would provide an institutional structure capable of bringing the truth of prior unity into life as a working-principle, and, thus, restoring to the Earth-system (both human and non-human) its inherent capability to self-correct and self-organize. In summary, the Global Cooperative Forum would deal with the issues that affect Earthkind as a whole—through a global cooperative process of self-governance on the part of the people of the world.

—Carolyn Lee

No Enemies

The pattern of world politics that has been dramatized with increasing intensity over time—and with the most devastating effects in the twentieth century, with the two devastating world wars and all the other wars right up to the present day—is based on the idea and the pattern of polar opposition. Therefore, the common political method is to have opposites either confront one another or (otherwise) try to work out some kind of a deal with one another.

As Abraham Lincoln said, "A house divided against itself cannot stand." If the world-system is based on opposites, it will inevitably self-destruct—by creating chaos along the lines of division (or mutual opposition).

There have been (and, no doubt, will continue to be) many efforts to create some kind of global resolution (or world peace) by bringing opposites together. But any such effort is inevitably bound to fail. Such an effort cannot succeed. It is simply not possible, in the "physics" of human affairs, for such an approach to succeed.

Unity cannot be achieved by combining opposites. Unity is the _prior_ condition, the condition that is always already the case. Prior unity makes all opposites obsolete. Therefore, it is prior unity that must be enacted, rather than any continuation of the pattern of oppositions.

The world-situation has now developed to the point that there is nothing further to expect but the global collapse that opposition will inevitably produce. Therefore, this is the critical moment to stop the play of opposites in the domain of world politics. The play of opposites must be replaced by the politics of prior unity—through the Global Cooperative Forum of everybody-all-at-once. Such is an absolute necessity. Otherwise, the play of polar opposites is going to become absolute destruction.

The principle of prior unity applies to all human endeavor, even to the integrity of a human body or a human personality. Unity is not the result of a play of opposites. Unity is the prior condition.

It is only when unity (or indivisibility) is the principle of life, of living, of action, that unity results. If division (or opposition) is presumed to be the case, more division will result. This is an absolute law. Once this is understood, it clarifies everything about right action and right life.

My address to all human issues—necessarily including what I am saying about world politics—is based on this fundamental principle: Reality Itself is a prior unity. Reality Itself is indivisible and egoless. Therefore, life must be lived in accordance with that Self-Nature of Reality Itself.

This absolute principle is fundamental to all resolution of human problems. In Gandhi's language, it is a "soul-force", or "truth-force", as he understood it.[11] That must be the force behind all political effort—the force of prior unity. The principle of prior unity determines a course of action that is (necessarily) inclusive of everybody-all-at-once. What is required is not a search for unity. Rather, what is required is the enacting of the power of prior unity. That is the principle. And it must be the governing principle of political action.

How should humankind deal with the world-situation? By enacting the principle of prior unity. And an instrument is required in order to do that. That instrument is the Global Cooperative Forum. The Global Cooperative Forum must make obsolete all play-of-opposition in the world, all nation-state conflicts, all effort to size up great units of nation-states over against other such units, in the attempt to achieve victory over one another—one religion over another religion, one nation-state (or group of nation-states) over another nation-state (or group of nation-states), and so forth.

11. Gandhi's term was "satyagraha", often translated as "soul-force" or "truth-force", indicating Gandhi's insistence that the power of truth can (and should) be used as a non-violent means to effect change.

All of this effort to defeat the presumed opponent is insanity. Humankind cannot afford to go on with this. Humankind must stop this.

This is the decisive moment in human history to stop this, because such insanity cannot go on without total devastation being the result. Therefore, there truly is no choice.

Those who hear what I have to say about this will understand: There must be an active embrace of this understanding at every level of human life, including every matter associated with global politics and environmental issues. Everything at the human scale must be addressed on the basis of enacting the principle of prior unity, through instruments that are inclusive of everybody-all-at-once. It is essentially a matter of putting the Truth-principle (or Reality-principle) of prior unity into action. And an instrument is needed to do that—not just words.

It is not a matter of bringing together collectives of different groups—such as governmental organizations and non-governmental organizations—so that they can each have their voice, thereby playing out the chaos of oppositions. There is no time to be doing any such thing. There must be a different instrument—and everybody-all-at-once must volunteer for it and become active within it.

Humankind must wake up to its inherent and intrinsic unity as a whole, and not play on any differences whatsoever. Human beings must grasp this understanding of prior unity—and act on it, through an appropriate instrument that is altogether full of integrity and altogether right. That is the immediate necessity associated with bringing the Global Cooperative Forum into being.

Wherever action is done in opposition to whatever force or entity is considered to be the opponent, wherever there is even a strategy relative to an opponent, the effort will fail. Some kinds of changes may be brought about—but, ultimately, everything stays the same, because the principle is one of division to begin with.

Likewise, every strategy that is developed in opposition to any force whatsoever will inevitably fail. The only principle that can work politically is one in which there is no opponent and no search to defeat an opponent—and, therefore, fundamentally no struggle. Right human politics is simply about enacting—or asserting and carrying out—the principle of prior unity.

That kind of activism does not presume an opponent. It does not involve itself with self-division. Consequently, it will not fail. In contrast, whatever presumes its own self-division will fail. It will only produce more division. Therefore, the only kind of political action that can possibly achieve ultimate success is activism based on (1) the presumption of prior unity and (2) the enactment of prior unity through an appropriate instrument.

There is nobody "else". There is no opponent. The Global Cooperative Forum is a means for bypassing all oppositions, all opposites, and the entire game that plays upon there being opposites at all. There should be presumed to be no opposites, no enemies, no opponent to be defeated. There is simply the intrinsic fact of prior unity. Right politics is simply about acting on that basis.

That is what the Global Cooperative Forum must do. And that is what the form of global activism I am describing must do. That is how it must function: no enemies, no game in opposition, and (therefore) no strategy in relation to a presumed opponent—none.

That is the profundity at the root of such activism—the intensive presumption of non-separateness, of prior unity, of no opponent, of no self-division. That is the only right and effective strategy. It is not a goal-seeking strategy. It is a matter of enacting a prior reality, rather than seeking a different reality. Such is the unique understanding that is the root of all true wisdom.

When I am speaking about politics, I am looking at it in the context of humankind-as-a-whole—not in terms of any circumstance that is negative, full of opposites, looking to achieve some kind of a victory in relation to an opposite or an opponent or an enemy. The root-presumption of not having an enemy is essential to the Global Cooperative Forum. The Global Cooperative Forum must be intrinsically all-including. And there is a discipline necessary for doing that, because people's patterning will tend to have them be expressing opposite views, different dispositions, and wanting to just sit around and talk about all of that. There should be absolutely no discussion of that kind. That has nothing to do with anything.

There is nothing but Reality Itself—the prior whole, the indivisible whole. That is the basis for all right action. All right human action must be based on this understanding.

In one of the Upanishads, it is said that wherever there is an "other", fear arises.[12] As soon as "difference" is presumed, as soon as separateness is presumed, as soon as an opponent is presumed, there is fear—or the disposition of separativeness, of self-protectiveness, of self-division. The non-presumption of an "other" is the essential principle that will liberate humankind. Wherever no "other" is presumed, Truth awakens.

That is the significance of the title of the book *Not-Two Is Peace*. What I describe in that book is not merely a method for seeking peace. All twoness is about a search toward a goal—including the goal of peace, which idealists want to find someday. What I am proposing is not idealism. Rather, it is perfect realism—in relation to politics, and in relation to every other domain of human life. Such realism involves the intensive non-presumption of "other" and "problem". Such realism is the "not-two" presumption—thoroughly embraced, and become the basis of action. That

12. In S. Radhakrishnan's translation of the Brhadaranyaka Upanishad, this sentence reads: "Assuredly it is from a second that fear arises," where "second" is used in the sense of "other" [S. Radhakrishnan, ed., *The Principal Upanishads* (Atlantic Highlands, NJ: Humanities Press, 1992), 164].

action is <u>already</u> characterized by unity—not the search for unity, but the <u>Is</u>-ness of unity.

Such is the right basis for all human activism. Indeed, it is the basis for all right action in every domain of human life. And this understanding is how everything can be made right, now and in the future. It is the Wisdom-means that can (and must) be applied in the case of every human process. Therefore, it applies to everything—including the most inclusive of all possibilities, which is the right functioning of humankind-as-a-whole.

This is a call to everyone to be awakened to an <u>intrinsic</u> understanding. It is not about appealing to people as egos, or merely trying to get everybody together, with all their differences, to simply talk things out. It is not about anything like that. It is about completely bypassing all of that. All of that will fail. It is a waste of time—and there is no time to be wasted. Rather, this call to everyone is about presuming the intrinsic Truth-intuition (or Reality-intuition) in everyone, rather than appealing to people as consumer-egos or egos-in-high-places.

The principle of non-violence is an idealistic principle about how to function in relation to an opponent. What I am communicating is not that. The principle of "Not-Two <u>Is</u> Peace" is not a strategy in relation to an opponent. In fact, it is <u>exactly</u> <u>not</u> that. Thus, the principle of "Not-Two <u>Is</u> Peace" is not the principle of non-violence merely, even though it is thoroughly and intrinsically non-violent. Most fundamentally, the principle of "Not-Two <u>Is</u> Peace" is about not using any method that presumes to be in relation to an opponent.

All actions done in relation to an opponent—even if outwardly non-violent—are, in some sense, violent. That needs to be understood. Any struggle with an opponent is a kind of aggression, even if done through the device of non-violence.

The approach of "Not-Two <u>Is</u> Peace" (with the Global Cooperative Forum as its instrument) is not like that. It is not an effort in relation to an opponent. It is simply everybody-all-at-once becoming self-actualizing, self-enforcing, self-governing, self-rightening, self-correcting, self-organizing, not opposing anything. It is the whole-all-at-once putting itself in order, as it will inevitably do when the obstruction that is preventing that self-organizing process from happening is removed.

Thus, it is oppositions that are preventing the self-organizing process from happening. The idea of "difference" is what is preventing humankind from self-organizing and self-correcting and self-rightening itself. That is it. The presumption of "difference", the presumption of opposites, of opponents, of necessary struggle, of seeking for unity, of winning against some force or other that is the opposite of your own—that is what is wrong.

This is the unique understanding that people must grasp. The lack of that understanding is the reason why humankind is defeating itself. That is why worthy purposes are failing. It is the presumption of "difference", the presumption of the "other", the presumption of "not yet—therefore, seeking is required".

In other words, the presumption of egoity or the presumption of separateness and the activity of separation— is the fault that makes all human effort fail. Ego is the "difference"-maker. Ego is the separatist (or separative) disposition. Ego ultimately avoids relationship, dissociating itself from the "other". Therefore, the dissociative principle must be abandoned. It has nothing to do with peace. It has nothing to do with correcting the human situation.

All action based on the presumption of an "other" or of "difference" will inevitably fail. Such action only produces struggle, and not unity. Truly, it could be said that the entire world has engaged in its political efforts at the cost of destroying global unity. The United Nations functions on the basis of opposites or differences. It is based on bringing competitors or opponents together in one place, where they continue to be opponents and competitors in relation to one another. They sit around talking, but such talk has nothing to do with peace, with the unity and well-being of humankind-as-a-whole. Talk will never achieve peace or unity or well-being.

The Global Cooperative Forum is an intrinsically unified body representing everybody-all-at-once. Therefore, there are no differences in it. It is not about a council of nations. It is simply a working-instrument for the priorly unified totality (or whole) of humankind, and it presumes no differences.

Therefore, all name-tags and placards must be abandoned at the door. You do not bring your nation-state labels (or any other labels) inside. There are no "high" persons. There are no differences. There is no status. All are servants of the whole.

This is not mere idealism. This is Reality in action. It is an absolute necessity. It always has been—but it has never been understood in the context of humankind-as-a-whole, because humankind-as-a-whole never came together before. That coming-together is only a recent happening.

Thus, in the Global Cooperative Forum, it cannot be that the different nations, the different religions, the different cultures, the different races are each having their say, trying to "angle" relative to the interests on their side. The basis for coming together must be the principle of the human totality as a prior unity—bringing no differences to the table whatsoever, but simply bringing the subjects of address that are common to all, and collectively solving those issues through action that is appropriate to whatever particular subject.

To do that, all presumptions of "difference" must be abandoned. That is the principle of the Global Cooperative Forum.

As I have already described, the principle of prior unity as a political means is not the same as the strategy of non-violent aggression in relation to an opponent. It is quite different—and that difference must be understood. What I am communicating is something new. It is not in the likeness of anything that has previously been proposed or enacted. Sympathetic associations can be seen in the history of human efforts toward peace, but the principle of prior unity is not the same as any previous principle for establishing peace. What is unique about the principle of prior unity must be thoroughly grasped and intensively applied.

The potential of sanity is always priorly the case.

Now sanity must come to the front.

Human beings must now presume to act and live in the inherently sane manner of prior unity—and of the Indivisible Prior Truth That Is Reality Itself.

—Adi Da
July 23, 2007

EPILOGUE

The Great Project

"Not-two" is peace.
"Not-two" is prior unity.
Conversely, "two" is separateness,
    prior dis-unity, "difference", otherness,
    competitiveness, opposition, confrontation,
    chaos, and war.

In the "room" of humankind as a whole,
the "room" of everybody-all-at-once,
there is no "two"—
    there are no "flags",
    there are no religions,
    and there is no "self"-imagery
        that may be exclusively asserted.
Rather, humankind must simply represent itself,
    and get together to create a new global domain
    for human existence.

This is the great project.

Adi Da at his island-hermitage in Fiji, 2003

THE WORLD-FRIEND ADI DA

From his birth (on Long Island, New York, in 1939), Adi Da always manifested unique signs of spiritual illumination. Nevertheless, from his birth, and until his spiritual restoration at thirty years of age, Adi Da submitted himself to an ordeal of "self-identification" with all the limitations and sufferings of the human condition.[13]

Adi Da describes his early years as being focused in two fundamental activities: investigating how, in the scale of human "ordinariness", to perfectly realize the Truth of "Reality Itself", and (coincidently) both achieving and demonstrating the human-scale ability to communicate the Truth of "Reality Itself" through both visual and verbal means.

Adi Da graduated from Columbia University in 1961, with a BA in philosophy, and from Stanford University in 1966, with an MA in English literature. His master's thesis, a study of core issues in modernism, focused on the literary experiments of Gertrude Stein and on the modernist painters of the same period.

In 1964, Adi Da began a period of intensive practice under a succession of spiritual masters in the United States and India. In 1968, he went to India and approached the renowned spiritual master Swami Muktananda of Ganeshpuri, who immediately responded by saying that Adi Da was a spiritual master at birth, and "the most extraordinary Westerner" he (Swami Muktananda) had ever encountered. One year later, in a unique letter of acknowledgment, Swami Muktananda made an open public declaration that Adi Da, by virtue of his evident spiritual signs and demonstrated states, was inherently qualified to teach others independently,

---

13. For Adi Da's autobiographical account of his life and work, please see *The Knee of Listening* (Middletown, CA: The Dawn Horse Press, 2004).

and to awaken others spiritually by direct transmission. Later, in 1970, after a final period of intense spiritual endeavor, Adi Da spontaneously became re-established in the continuous state of illumination that was his unique condition at birth.

After his re-awakening, Adi Da began to teach, creating a vast repository of wisdom, in living dialogue with those who approached him as devotees. His literary, philosophical, and practical writings consist of over seventy published books— many internationally acclaimed. In the early 1970s, Alan Watts, writer of numerous books on religion and philosophy, acknowledged Adi Da as "a rare being", adding, "It is obvious, from all sorts of subtle details, that he knows what IT's all about." In the late 1990s, poet Robert Lax said of Adi Da's radically experimental novel, *The Mummery Book* (the opening volume of Adi Da's *Orpheum* trilogy), "Living and working as a writer for many decades, I have not encountered a book like this, that mysteriously and unself-consciously conveys so much of the unspeakable reality."

Having fully given his teaching, Adi Da lived independently on his island hermitage in Fiji, constantly working to express the Truth of existence through modes of communication to which all human beings can respond—including literary, theatrical, artistic, and philosophical works. Simultaneously, and most fundamentally, he was always working to establish his island-hermitage as a place from which his spiritual blessing could perpetually flow into the world, both during and after his physical lifetime. He passed from the body on November 27, 2008.

Adi Da is not political in any ordinary sense of the word. Rather, his address to humanity and the process of civilization comes from his lifelong intention of communicating the truth of existence—uncovering both the essential driving forces of limitation and suffering and the means to go beyond those forces. ■

GLOSSARY

acausal—Neither caused nor causing; therefore, existing beyond (or prior to) the realm of duality in which the law of "cause and effect" is operative.

conditionally manifested existence—The reality we ordinarily perceive and participate in, which is a complex effect of all kinds of causes. This "ordinary existence" can manifest only in accordance with whatever conditions are the case. Because "ordinary existence" is dependent on conditions, Adi Da describes it as "conditionally manifested". He contrasts this with "Reality Itself" (which is intrinsically "non-conditional"). See also **Conscious Light** and **Reality Itself**.

Conscious Light—Adi Da defines Reality (Itself) as "Conscious Light". By making this definition, he is communicating that the two essential characteristics of Reality are Awareness (or Consciousness) and Radiance (or Light, or Energy). Furthermore, Adi Da states that Conscious Light is the essential nature (or the "One and Only Self-Nature, Self-Condition, and Self-State") of every thing and every being in the universe.

"dark" epoch—See **"late-time" (or "dark" epoch)**.

"difference"—Adi Da defines the presumption of fundamental "difference" as the essential fault that characterizes the unliberated human ego. The core of this presumption is the primal notion that "self" is separate from "everything and everyone else". That primal notion is described by Adi Da as the "root" of all human suffering and dilemma.

ecstasy—The word "ecstasy", derived from the Greek, means "standing (stasis) outside (ec-)". Adi Da uses this word with the specific meaning of "standing outside the egoic 'self'" (a condition which is inherently blissful).

ego / egoity / ego-"I"—Adi Da teaches that the ego is an activity, and not an entity. The activity of egoity is what Adi Da calls the "'self'-contraction", or the presumption of separate and separative existence. When he uses the term "ego-'I'", he places the "I" in quotation marks to indicate that he uses it in the "so to speak" sense. He is indicating (by means of the quotation marks) that, in Reality, there is no such thing as the "I", even though it seems to be the case in ordinary experience.

egolessness—Adi Da uses this term to mean "the condition of freedom from the presumption of a separate and separative existence", or "the condition of freedom from the presumption of separate 'point of view'".

end-time—A reference to the present time, where the presumption and activity of separateness has brought humanity to the nadir of civilization, and to the point of ultimate destructiveness. In using this term, Adi Da is not making reference to any of the traditional religious myths of an apocalyptic end-time. See also **"late-time" (or "dark" epoch)**.

Enlightenment—The actual Realization of Reality Itself, or Truth Itself—which Realization is inherently full of Light.

everybody-all-at-once—A phrase coined by Adi Da indicating the "all-at-once collective" of humanity—which is not a collection of separate individuals, but the force of humankind as a collective whole, based in the fundamental presumption and truth of prior unity.

gross—Adi Da most often uses "gross" with its meaning of "made up of material (or physical) elements". The gross (or physical) dimension of existence is (thus) associated with the physical body and world.

"ground zero"—A term coined in the twentieth century to describe the site where an explosion (especially a nuclear one) has occurred. Since September 11, 2001, this term has also commonly been used to refer to the site of the destroyed World Trade Center in New York City. In this book, Adi Da uses this term as a metaphor for the state of global human culture at this time in history.

"late-time" (or "dark" epoch)—Adi Da uses the terms "late-time" and "'dark' epoch" to describe the present era, in which doubt of anything at all beyond mortal existence is more and more pervading the entire world, and the self-interest of the separate individual is more and more regarded to be the ultimate principle of life.

"objectification"—Adi Da consistently places the words "object", "objective", "objectify", "objectification", and so forth, in quotation marks. He does this in order to indicate that the common presumption that "object" and "subject" are inherently separate is, in truth, illusory.

"point of view"—By placing this phrase in quotation marks, Adi Da is communicating that, in Reality, every "point of view" is an illusion—because all "point of view" is founded in the presumption that "I" exist separate from everyone and everything else.

prior unity—Adi Da's term "prior unity" is not pointing to some past "golden age" of unity on Earth. Rather, Adi Da is speaking of the inherent, or "a priori", unity of existence—the primal, irreducible state of being in which the world and all things continually arise and pass away. This original state of being is, by its very nature, one and indivisible, regardless of the apparently separate happenings that arise within it. This can be understood by looking at the ocean, which is a single body of water supporting an ever-changing pattern of individual waves. The principle of prior unity is demonstrated ever more in the domains of physics (in terms of the understanding of matter as a unified continuum of energy) and biology (in terms of even the shared genetic structure of human beings). Thus, Adi Da's term "prior unity" points to the unity that exists prior to all the apparent differences and conflicts in the world. That unity, in other words, is senior to all apparent signs of disunity. Adi Da also calls this the "unifying life-principle" and the "cosmically extended pattern of oneness". Adi Da is pointing out—in this book and elsewhere—that a clear awareness of the truth of prior unity enables intelligent collective action—action that starts from the working-principle that prior unity is already so, rather than action that "works toward" or struggles to establish unity.

"radical"—Derived from the Latin "radix" (meaning "root"), "radical" principally means "irreducible", "fundamental", or "relating to the origin". Thus, Adi Da defines "radical" as "at-the-root". Because Adi Da uses "radical" in this literal sense, it appears in quotation marks in his writings, in order to distinguish his usage from the common reference to an extreme (often political) view.

Reality Itself—In contrast to "conditionally manifested existence", Adi Da refers to "Reality Itself" (with capital letters). Reality Itself is not in any sense dependent on conditions. In other words, Reality Itself is utterly "non-conditional". Adi Da states that Reality Itself is the "One and Only Self-Nature, Self-Condition, and Self-State" of every thing and every being in the universe.

Real-God-Realization—Adi Da uses the term "Real God" to refer to Reality or Truth Itself, rather than any conventional anthropomorphic idea of God as "Creator". "Real-God-Realization" can be of various kinds and degrees, depending on the esoteric tradition in which such Realization appears.

"self" / not-"self"—The two categories of egoic illusion: that which one identifies with ("self"), and everything else (not-"self"). Adi Da places "self" in quotation marks to indicate that the presumption of a separate entity is an illusion—generated in response to the fact of bodily existence.

"self"-fulfillment—Ultimate and permanent happiness and satisfaction for the separate "self", which Adi Da defines as an inherently unattainable goal.

separative / separativeness—The inclination to maintain one's presumed state of separateness from everyone and everything else.

"tribal" / "tribalism" / "tribes"—Adi Da uses these terms to refer to the ego in its collective form. Please see p. 21 for a full discussion.

World-Friend—See p. 17.

FOR FURTHER STUDY

Many of the readings in Prior Unity *are found in their fullest form in Adi Da's books* Not-Two <u>Is</u> Peace *and* Transcendental Realism.[14] *The following list indicates where the reader may find the full texts of the essays in these two books (and also in two separate booklet publications).*

The remaining readings in Prior Unity *(which are not included in the list below) are, for the most part, previously unpublished communications by Adi Da.*

---

14. In *Transcendental Realism*, Adi Da discusses the body of artwork he created (as a means of making a non-verbal communication about reality), as well as the significance of art in general (and modernist art in particular) relative to human civilization. *Transcendental Realism* and the booklets listed on p. 121 are published by the Dawn Horse Press, Middletown, CA.

PART TWO: WHAT MUST BE DONE
- The Retrieval of Inspired Culture
  See "The Eternal War Between Orpheus and Narcissus" (*Transcendental Realism*, pp. 175–82)
- Vibratory Participation
  See "The Beautiful Room of Perfect Space" (*Transcendental Realism*, pp. 159–69)
- Cooperative, Human-Scale Community
  See *Cooperative, Human-Scale Community and the Integrity (Religious, and Altogether) of Civilization* (booklet)
- No Longer Exploitable
  See "Reality-Politics For Ordinary Men and Women" (*Not-Two Is Peace*, pp. 117–29)
- The Fundamental Domain At The Center Of Life
  See *My Call for the Universal Restoration of the Sacred (or Central) Domain of Human Life* (booklet)
- The "Everybody Force"
  See "Everybody-All-At-Once" (*Not-Two Is Peace*, pp. 181–94)

EPILOGUE
The Great Project
  See "On The Dangers of The Old 'Tribalisms', and The Necessity For A Global Cooperative Forum Based On The Prior Unity of Humankind" (*Not-Two Is Peace*, pp. 41–48)

INDEX

A

acausal change, 88
action, right
　via identification with the totality of humankind, 52
　love as, 63
　"not-two" presumption as basis for, 105–7
　of people and corporations, 93
　prior unity as basis for, 41–42, 102–3, 110
　by tapping human urge for participation, 61
activism, universal
　discipline of, 105
　of everybody-all-at-once, 25
　prior unity as basis for, 104, 106
Adi Da
　artwork of, 27
　biography of, 115–16
　on cooperative community, 22
　"everybody-all-at-once" as proposed by, 24–25
　Global Cooperative Forum as proposed by, 99
　on prior unity, 13
　on separative ego-activity, 19–20
　spiritual work of coincidence with the world, 16, 17
　work to righten human culture, 31
　as World-Friend, 17
animal protein dependency, 81–83
animals, 83
arts, the, 69

B

Beauty, 60
Berlin Wall, fall of the, 15, 25
Burke, Leo, 14

C

change
　of consciousness to address totality, 31
　corporate power to effect, 92, 93
　via force of everybody-all-at-once, 86, 88, 89
　morphic fields theory on collective, 20
　as served by *Prior Unity* book, 13, 18
chaos
　of dis-united collective, 86, 87
　of ego-power, 89, 90
　of opposites in confrontation, 101, 103
　"self"-fulfillment myth as the source of, 86
　of "tribal" confrontation, 48
　of "two", 113
　wilderness mythology of the totality as, 78
civilization
　Adi Da's call for unity-based, 17–18

cooperative community as basis for, 22–23, 63
　principles for survivable, 94
　separative worldview of current, 13
　transformation of, 13, 25
climate change, 81, 82, 83
collective
　"everybody force" of the, 86
　individuals as influencing the, 20–21
　laws of function within the, 77–78
　as reflective of individuals, 81
　responsibility, 84
　self-awareness as the, 24–25, 51–52
　See also everybody-all-at-once
community
　cooperative, human-scale, 22, 63
　as fundamental human urge, 62
　love as the key to, 63
　principal "food" of, 64
　responsibility as required by, 65
　sacred domain as accessed via, 70–71
competition, 79, 113
conflict
　of identities, 39
　as no longer applicable, 96
　of opposites, 101
　separateness as root of, 21
　"tribalism" as, 46–48, 78–80
　See also opposition
consciousness
　of everybody-all-at-once, 24–25
　presumption of separative, 19–20
　prior unity as real nature of, 20
　requirement for unity-based, 42
　shift to recognize the world-as-totality, 78–80
Consciousness Itself, 37, 64
consumer mentality, 61, 106
control of ecstasy, 68–69
cooperation
　brings order to global totality, 79
　in community, 22, 63
　by corporate powers, 92–93
　existence as based on, 16
　as fundamental human urge, 62
　global process as based on, 48–49
　love as key to, 63
　necessity for, 42
　sacred domain of, 71
　State as following human example of, 65–66
　survivable civilization as based on, 84, 94
corporations
　complicity in fossil fuel and animal protein dependencies, 82
　cooperative, rightening power of, 92–93
　policy changes necessary for, 84, 85

re-orienting, 93
"tribalism" among, 21, 79
negotiation, 24
non-human beings, 83
non-separation, 16, 19, 40
non-violence, 106, 108–9
Not-Two Is Peace, 24, 99, 105
"Not-Two Is Peace" principle, 105–7, 113

O

Oculus One: The Reduction of The Beloved, 27
opposition
 inevitable failure of, 103–4
 non-presumption of, 105–7
 politics of, 101
 as presumption of dis-unity, 102
 as "two", 113
 United Nations as based on, 107–8
 See also conflict; "tribalism"

P

paradigms, new and old, 53, 99
participation, 61
parts within a whole, 41
pattern
 of opposition, 105
 of participation, 61
 similarity of individual and collective, 81
peace
 golden rule as insufficient for, 21
 "not-two" is, 105–7
 opposites cannot achieve, 108
 prior unity as enabling, 25, 109
"point of view", 51–52, 118
politics
 of dis-unity, 86
 of opposites in confrontation, 101, 107–8
 of prior unity, 101, 102, 104, 108
 true basis for, 19, 62
pollution, 81, 82
power
 of corporations and people, 92–93
 of everybody-all-at-once, 86, 88, 90
prior unity
 as already so, 16, 34
 cooperative community as expressing, 22
 Earth's issues as viewed from, 83
 egolessness of, 40
 enacting, 102, 103, 104
 Global Cooperative Forum as governance
  via, 99–100, 108
 as guiding, rightening source, 50
 life based on the presumption of, 39
 makes all opposites obsolete, 101
 "not-two" is, 113

as peace, 109
Reality Itself is, 19, 37, 38, 80
 as realized by everybody-all-at-once, 87
 re-asserting power of, 89, 90
 sane action based on, 110
 as seniority of the whole to the parts, 41
 visual image of, 27
 working-presumption of, 20, 42, 90, 100
*Prior Unity: The Basis For A New Human
  Civilization*
 cooperation as expounded in, 16
 cover image, 27
 as distillation of Adi Da's wisdom, 17–18
 new worldview as served by, 13
 prophetic call in, 19
profundity, 60, 68, 104
public domain. *See* secular domain

R

Rang Avadhoot, Sri, 17
Real-God-Realization, 68, 69, 119
realism, 60, 90, 105
reality
 as a non-dual paradox, 68
 prior unity as source-, 19
 true context of, 37, 38
Reality Itself
 in action, 108
 giving voice and power to, 89
 human need to participate in, 60
 as indivisible Truth, 110
 as investigated by Adi Da, 115
 is a prior unity, 37, 38, 80, 102
 is all there is, 105
 love as participation in, 63
responsibility
 for community, 62
 of everybody-all-at-once, 50, 88
 individual and collective, 84
 to manage the collective totality, 78–80
 as required in community, 65
 to self-righten the world, 89
rightening
 as acausal, 88
 by corporate powers, 92–93
 by everybody-all-at-once, 87, 89
 as lifetime work of Adi Da, 31
 prior unity as guide for, 50
root-intelligence, 16

S

sacred domain
 as ecstatic core of life, 68–69, 70
 elements of, 69–70
 sanity via restoration of, 70–71

sanity, 70, 110
science, 13, 38, 68
secular domain, 67–69, 70–71
seeking, 107
"self"
 -fulfillment, as goal at root of global chaos,
  86–87
 -identity, as subordinate to collective, 51–52
 -sacrifice, 64
 separative presumption of, 19–20
self-conversion, 88
self-organizing principle
 of everybody-all-at-once, 88–89, 107
 of the Global Cooperative Forum, 99, 100
 prior unity as basis for, 90
separation/separateness
 cooperation as relinquishing, 51–52
 current worldview as based on, 13
 destructive darkness of, 40
 as a false presumption, 107
 golden rule as presuming, 21
 governance based on, 24
 as no longer applicable, 96
 parts within a whole as, 41
 self and world as presumed in, 19–20, 51
 "tribalism" as, 47
 as "two", 113
sex, 68, 69
Sheldrake, Rupert, 21
social contract, 18, 19
society
 establishment of a global, 47
 governance serving the totality of, 23–24
 laws of function within, 77–78
 prior unity presumption as basis of, 39
 See also culture, human
State, the, 65–66; See also governments
stress, 48

T

The Mummery Book, 116
*The Reduction of The Beloved To As Is (The
 Lover, The Bride, The Wife, The Widow)—
 Part Four: The Bride / 6*, 27
tolerance, 48–49, 94
totality
 applying order to, 77–78
 as domain of human responsibility, 79–80
 Global Cooperative Forum as servant of, 108
 identification with/as, 51–52
 prior unity of, 80
 rightening based on existing as, 50
 as wilderness, myth about, 78

toxic energy dependency, 84, 85
transformation, global
 beyond "tribalism", 21–22, 46–50
 to a culture of exceeding limit, 59
 from egoity to egolessness, 40
 via force of everybody-all-at-once, 86–88
 of humankind-as-a-whole, 46–47
 necessity for, 18, 31
 to a new paradigm, 53
 to "Not-Two Is Peace" principle, 105–7, 113
 via restoration of the sacred domain, 69–71
 from separativeness to unity, 13, 25
"tribalism"
 as collective egoity, 21
 competitive worldview of, 79
 as identity-and-difference, 48
 as a mechanism of pollution, 81
 necessity to transcend, 46–50
 as the old paradigm, 53
 as potential pitfall in community, 22
Truth Itself
 as communicated by Adi Da, 115, 116
 human necessity to participate in, 60
 as non-presumption of difference, 105–6
 Reality Itself as, 110
twentieth century, 31, 46

U

United Nations, 24, 99, 107
universe, the, 13
Upanishads, 105
urbanization, 62
utopia, 67, 68, 84

W

war, 79, 113
Watts, Alan, 116
whole, unity of parts within a, 41
wilderness, the, 78
world, the
 cooperative communities of, 22–23
 as presumed separate from self, 19–20
 root of current difficulty in, 84
 See also Earth
World-Friend Adi Da, 17